Classifying Living Things

Reptiles

Richard and Louise Spilsbury

Heinemann
LIBRARY

Chicago, Illinois

www.heinemannraintree.com
Visit our website to find out
more information about
Heinemann-Raintree books.

To order:

☎ Phone 888-454-2279

🖥 Visit www.heinemannraintree.com
to browse our catalog and order online.

© 2003, 2009 Heinemann Library
an imprint of Capstone Global Library, LLC
Chicago, Illinois

Customer Service: 888-454-2279

Visit our website at www.heinemannraintree.com

Edited by Catherine Clarke and Claire Throp
Designed by Victoria Bevan and AMR Design, Ltd.
Original illustrations © Capstone Global Library, LLC.
Illustrations by David Woodroffe
Picture research by Hannah Taylor

Printed and bound in China by Leo Paper Group

13 12 11 10 09
10 9 8 7 6 5 4 3 2 1

Library of Congress Cataloging-in-Publication Data

Spilsbury, Louise.
   Classifying reptiles / Louise and Richard Spilsbury.
p. cm. -- (Classifying living things)
Summary: Explains what reptiles are and how they differ from
others animals, offering an overview of the life cycle of a variety
of reptiles, including snakes, turtles, lizards, and crocodiles.
Includes bibliographical references (p.   ) and index.
   ISBN 978-1-4329-2357-0 (lib. bdg. : hardcover) -- ISBN 978-
1-4329-2367-9 (pbk.)
   1. Reptiles--Classification--Juvenile literature. 2. Reptiles--
Juvenile literature. [1. Reptiles.] I. Spilsbury, Richard, 1963- II.
Title. III Series.
   QL645 .S65 2003
   597.9--dc21
                                    2002015399

Acknowledgments

For Harriet and Miles, slow-worm enthusiasts.

We would like to thank the following for permission to
reproduce photographs: Corbis pp. 16 (Michael & Patricia
Fogden), 24 (Peter Johnson), 19 (Gallo Images/Anthony
Bannister); FLPA pp. 13 (Minden Pictures/Konrad Wothe),
20 (Albert Visage), 23 (Minden Pictures/Chris Newbert),
29 (Roger Tidman); naturepl pp. 5 (Georgette Douwma), 26
(David Kjaer), 28 (Jose B. Ruiz); NHPA pp. 4 (Daniel Zupanc),
8 (Lady Philippa Scott), 9 (James Carmichael Jr), 14 (A.N.T.),
15 (Stephen Dalton), 25 (Daniel Heuclin); Photolibrary pp.
6, 21 (OSF), 10 (OSF/Tui De Roy), 11 (OSF/Philippe Henry),
12 (OSF/George Bryce), 17 (OSF/Brian Kenney), 18 (John
Cancalosi), 22 (OSF/Godfrey Merlen); Photoshot p. 27
(Eye Ubiquitous).

Cover photograph of a marine iguana with a lava lizard
on its head, on the Galapagos Islands, reproduced with
permission of naturepl/Kerstin Hinze.

We would like to thank Ann Fullick for her invaluable
assistance in the preparation of this book.

Contents

Some words are shown in bold, **like this**. You can find out what they mean by looking in the glossary.

The natural world is full of an incredible variety of **organisms**. They range from tiny bacteria, too small to see, to giant redwood trees over 100 meters (330 feet) tall. With such a bewildering variety of life, it is hard to make sense of the living world. For this reason, scientists classify living things by sorting them into groups.

Classifying the living world

Sorting organisms into groups makes them easier to understand. Scientists try to classify living things in a way that tells you how closely one group is related to another. They look at everything about an organism, from its color and shape to the **genes** inside its **cells**. They even look at **fossils** to give them clues about how living things have changed over time. Then the scientists use all this information to sort the millions of different things into groups.

Scientists do not always agree about the group an organism belongs to, so they collect as much evidence as possible to find its closest relatives.

The body of a crocodile is one typical reptile shape. Other reptile groups, such as snakes or turtles, have different shapes.

From kingdoms to species

Classification allows us to measure the **biodiversity** of the world. To begin the classification process, scientists divide living things into huge groups called **kingdoms**. For example, plants are in one kingdom, while animals are in another. There is some argument among scientists about how many kingdoms there are—at the moment most agree that there are five! Each kingdom is then divided into smaller groups called **phyla** (singular *phylum*), and the phyla are further divided into **classes**. The next subdivision is into **orders**. Within an order, organisms are grouped into **families** and then into a **genus** (plural *genera*), which contains a number of closely related **species**. A species is a single type of organism, such as a mouse or a buttercup. Members of a species can **reproduce** and produce fertile offspring together.

Scientific names

Many living things have a common name, but these can cause confusion when the same organism has different names around the world. To avoid problems, scientists give every species a two-part Latin name, which is the same all over the world. The first part of the scientific name tells you the genus the organism belongs to. The second part tells you the exact species. The land iguana, for example, has the scientific name *Conolophus subcristatus*, while the marine iguana is *Amblyrhynchus cristatus*.

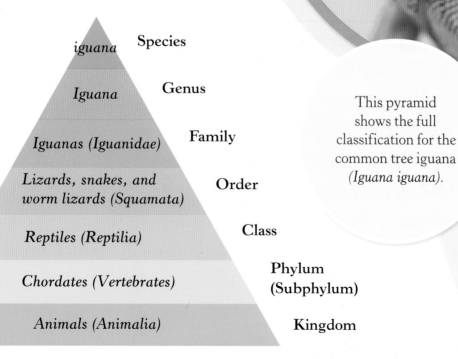

This pyramid shows the full classification for the common tree iguana (*Iguana iguana*).

iguana	Species
Iguana	Genus
Iguanas (Iguanidae)	Family
Lizards, snakes, and worm lizards (Squamata)	Order
Reptiles (Reptilia)	Class
Chordates (Vertebrates)	Phylum (Subphylum)
Animals (Animalia)	Kingdom

Reptiles come in many shapes, sizes, and colors, from giant armored crocodiles and tortoises to brightly colored lizards and snakes. No matter how different reptiles look, they all share a number of characteristics that distinguish them from other types of animals:

- They are **vertebrates**.
- Their skin is covered by hard, protective **scales**.
- They **reproduce** through eggs, which they lay on land.
- They breathe oxygen (a gas in the air) using lungs.
- They are **ectotherms**—they cannot control their own body temperature, so their bodies are always as hot or cold as their surroundings.

Types of reptiles

Reptiles are classified by their body structure—both inside and out. The main reptile groups are lizards, snakes, turtles, and crocodiles. Lizards usually have four limbs, long bodies, and tails. Snakes always have no limbs. Turtles and tortoises have a bony shell covering their backs. Crocodiles look a bit like lizards, but with long, toothed jaws and heavily armored skin.

There are two other groups of reptiles. The first contains only one **species**, the tuatara, which looks like a lizard. Members of the other group—the amphisbaenids, or worm lizards—look like snakes. These groups are classified separately because they have different skeletons than other reptiles.

It is clear that snakes are vertebrates if we look at their skeletons.

This table shows the **orders** of reptiles and gives some examples of main **families** and species.

Order	Suborder	Families	No. of species	Examples
Squamata (lizards, snakes, and amphisbaenids)	Lizards (Sauria)	Agamids (Agamidae)	300	frilled dragon
		Anguids (Anguidae)	75	slow-worm
		Beaded lizards (Helodermatidae)	2	Gila monster
		Chameleons (Chamaeleonidae)	85	Jackson's chameleon
		Geckos (Gekkonidae)	800	leopard gecko
		Iguanas (Iguanidae)	650	green iguana
		Lacertids (Lacertidae)	200	viviparous lizard
		Monitors (Varanidae)	31	Komodo dragon
		Skinks (Scincidae)	1,275	blue-tailed skink
	Snakes (Serpentes)	Boas and pythons (Boidae)	60	anaconda, tree python
		Rear-fangs (Colubridae)	1,500	garter snake
		Cobras (Elapidae)	170	Indian cobra
		Sea snakes (Hydrophiidae)	50	dusky sea snake
		Blind snakes (Typhlopidae)	200	southern blind snake
		Vipers (Viperidae)	180	diamondback rattlesnake
Rynchocephalia (tuatara)		(Sphenodontidae)	2	northern tuatara
Crocodilia (crocodiles, alligators, and caimans)		Alligators (Alligatoridae)	8	American alligator
		Crocodiles (Crocodylidae)	14	Nile crocodile
		Gavial (Gavialidae)	1	gharial
Chelonia (reptiles with shells)	Turtles, tortoises, and terrapins (Cryptodira)	Marine turtles (Cheloniidae)	5	hawksbill turtle
		Snapping turtles (Chelydridae)	2	alligator snapper
		Freshwater turtles (Emydidae)	76	diamondback terrapin
		Tortoises (Testudinidae)	40	giant tortoise
		Soft-shell turtles (Trionychidae)	20	Florida soft-shell turtle
	Side-necked turtles (Pleurodira)	Snake-necks (Chelidae)	21	matamata
		Side-necks (Pelomedusidae)	14	twist-necked turtle

Reptiles live all over the world, except in the coldest regions. Many live successfully in hot desert conditions. Their skin is an important key to survival in such extreme conditions.

Reptile skin is dry and covered in **scales**. Scales are thick pieces of dead skin. Not all scales are the same. Scales can be as tough as the strong crests on crocodile backs or as delicate as the smooth scales of a corn snake.

Dry and warm

All scaly skin is tough enough to help protect reptiles' soft insides. It is also waterproof. This helps to stop water inside reptiles from being lost through evaporation (changing into water vapor), allowing them to live in dry places.

Scaly skin may keep water in, but it loses heat easily. Since they are **ectothermic**, reptiles need to **bask** to get enough energy to move. Crocodiles bask on warm riverbanks. Some lizards stand with their sides facing the sun. Snakes may coil up on warm earth. As with other animals, too much heat can damage a reptile's body. In very hot **habitats**, reptiles usually hide from the sun during the day.

Do you know ... why some reptiles shed their skin?

Lizards and snakes shed (discard and replace) their skin regularly when it gets old or worn. The skin of tortoises and crocodiles just gets thicker with larger scales as they grow.

Marine iguanas stand up to soak up energy from the sun after swimming in the cold sea.

Vertebrate variations

The name *reptile* comes from the Latin word *repere*, which means "crawling." Not all reptiles crawl, however. Reptiles have different-shaped skeletons because they live in different ways.

Like all **vertebrates**, reptiles have a backbone. This is a column of small bones, called vertebrae, that form a strong, flexible tube protecting the spinal nerves and supporting the body. The ribs are connected to the backbone and support the heart and lungs. The limbs and the muscles that move them are also connected to the backbone or spine.

The backbone is also connected to limbs for movement. Lizards and crocodiles have four short, angled legs, which carry their body just above the ground. Snakes move without legs. They have very flexible backbones connected to as many as 400 ribs. They slither along, twisting their bodies back and forth using strong muscles.

Most reptiles have teeth. Crocodiles have a mouthful, but some snakes have just a few inside their throats for gripping onto food as they swallow it. Reptiles have no chewing teeth, so they either swallow food whole or rip chunks off.

The scales on this rattlesnake's body are different sizes. Tough scales help protect the front of its head as it moves and catches food.

9

Reptiles **reproduce** on land by laying eggs. One of the biggest dangers for all young animals developing inside eggs on land is drying out. To prevent this, all reptile eggs have a tiny puddle of fluid inside them.

Reptile eggs

Reptile eggs come in different shapes and sizes. Some are shaped like big jelly beans, while others are like ping-pong balls, or even like bumpy carrots. Most reptile eggs are surrounded by a soft, leathery skin, but some, such as gecko eggs, have a hard shell similar to that of birds' eggs. Inside each egg is a delicate skin that the baby can breathe through, a bag of watery fluid, and a yolk (food) for the developing reptile. Reptile eggs are more delicate than birds' eggs. If you turn a turtle egg over, for example, the baby turtle inside will probably suffocate and die, because the special skin can easily get damaged.

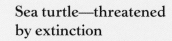

Sea turtle—threatened by extinction

- Large sea-dwelling reptile
- Always return to same beach to lay eggs
- Digs nest hole in sand with hind legs
- Lays hundreds of leathery shelled eggs and buries them before returning to sea
- Vulnerable to animal and human predators who dig up the eggs

Incubation and hatching

Reptile babies can only develop properly and hatch if their eggs stay at the right temperature. This is called **incubation**. Parent reptiles have different ways of making sure the eggs are warm enough. Alligators living by cool, shady riverbanks lay their eggs in mounds of leaves, which produce warmth as they rot. Pythons coil around their eggs and shiver their muscles to keep them warm.

Covering eggs to incubate them also hides them from **predators** such as egg-eating birds. Most female reptiles abandon their eggs once they are laid. Some, such as alligators, guard their eggs until they hatch. When reptiles hatch, they look like tiny versions of their parents, and most can take care of themselves right away.

Young alligators, like many other reptiles, have a special egg tooth on their upper jaw, which they use to cut their way out of their tough shell when they hatch.

Did you know ... some reptiles have live babies?

Some **species** of reptiles, such as pit vipers, incubate and hatch their eggs inside their bodies. Although this means the eggs have more protection, it also means these reptiles have fewer eggs, because there is not much room inside!

Lizards are the largest group of reptiles. They have distinct necks and tails, ear openings behind their eyes, and usually four legs. Although many lizards look a bit like crocodiles on the outside, they are similar to snakes on the inside. For example, like snakes they have sensitive pits in their mouths called Jacobson's **organ**, which they use to taste with. Lizards are therefore classified in the same **order** as snakes. Lizards, however, have fewer bones in their skulls than snakes.

The largest family

The skink **family** contains the largest number of **species** of all lizard families. Skinks are 15 to 30 centimeters (6 to 12 inches) long and live all over the world, usually on the ground or hidden in burrows. They are grouped together because they have no obvious neck and have smooth skin covered with shiny, rounded **scales**, broad tongues, scaly eyelids, and often very small legs.

Sand skinks live in hot desert **habitats**. They move just below the surface of the sand by wriggling their bodies from side to side. This is an easier way of getting around on shifting ground than walking on legs and toes.

The tails of many lizards break off easily so that they can escape from predators that have grabbed them. A new tail then grows. This skink has a blue tail to make sure predators go for its tail rather than its delicate head.

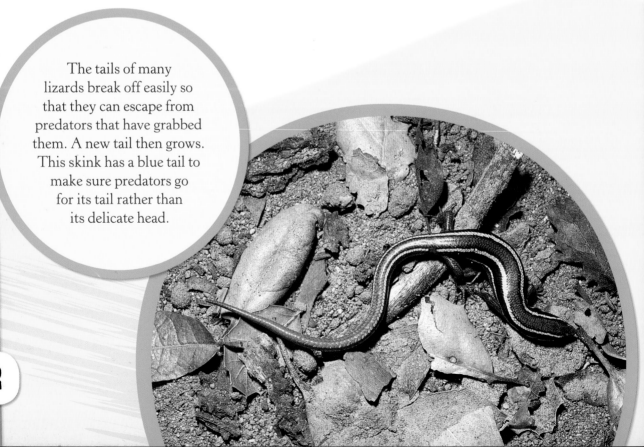

Sticking around

Geckos are small climbing lizards that live in warm parts of the world. They all have toes with ridged, bristle-covered pads and sharp claws, which make climbing easier. Geckos have no scales on their heads, and many have no eyelids. They clean their eyes by licking them!

Geckos are mainly **nocturnal** and catch and eat insects. They are very noisy, usually making repeated calls to let other geckos know where they are, or if **predators** are nearby.

Legless lizards

Several lizard families have no legs. This is an **adaptation** that helps them move through the thick grass and loose earth they live in. Despite their name, slow-worms are lizards, not worms—they have scaly bodies, hard skulls, and eyes with lids.

Tuatara—one of a kind
- Lives on islands near New Zealand
- Looks like a lizard
- Classified as a separate group due to the number of holes in the skull and the position of the teeth

The iguana group contains iguanas, agamids, and chameleons. These are all lizards with heavy bodies, short necks, fleshy tongues, and numerous belly **scales**. The other major group of lizards is the monitor group, which includes monitor lizards and bearded lizards. They have tiny, bumpy scales on their backs and forked tongues.

Iguanas and agamids

Iguanas are generally large lizards that live on land, up in trees, and even in the sea, in North, Central, and South America. Many male iguanas have crests and brightly colored throat fans that they display to attract females or to warn other males to stay away. Rhinoceros iguanas have thick scales like horns on their heads and a heavy build to avoid being hurt in fights.

Agamids live in different parts of the world from iguanas. Members of one **species**, frilled dragons, run away fast on their back legs when they see a possible **predator**. If cornered, they stretch open a frill of skin around their neck using special **cartilage** struts by their throat. The moloch—or thorny devil—is covered with thorn-like scales to scare off predators. If it is frightened it tucks its head in to become a prickly ball.

This frilled dragon is warning other animals to get away. It does this by spreading its frill, hissing, and moving toward them.

Hidden hunters

Chameleons look very different from iguanas and agamids because of their special **adaptations** for life in trees hunting for insect **prey**. They have a long, sticky tongue, eyes that can swivel in different directions, a prehensile (gripping) tail, and long legs with joined toes shaped like tongs, which they use to grip branches. Chameleons have **camouflaged** skin, which changes color if they move onto a different background. It also changes color with its mood—an angry chameleon turns black with rage.

Chameleon—color change specialist
- Eyes that swivel in different directions
- Feeds on insects
- Long tongue with sticky end to capture insects
- Prehensile tail
- Skin that changes color to match background and signal mood changes

The monitor group

Monitor lizards have long heads, sharp claws, and can swim well. They are sometimes massive—the Komodo dragon is a monitor that can reach 3 meters (10 feet) in length. It hides in dense forest on certain Indonesian islands, waiting to ambush prey such as wild boar and deer.

The gila monster and the beaded lizard live in hot deserts and are the only two poisonous lizards. Their backs have striking patterns of black, pink, or yellow scales. These markings warn other animals to keep away. If attacked, they bite and grip on while strong poison runs along grooves in their teeth into their victim.

Snakes are classified in the same **order** as lizards because they have similar skeletons. They are grouped in a different suborder from lizards because all snakes are different from lizards in several ways.

What are snakes?

Snakes have no legs, long bodies, and short tails. They have no ear openings. Instead of hearing, they sense movements around them, feeling vibrations through the ground. Instead of movable eyelids, they have transparent **scales** to protect their eyes. All snakes are carnivores (meat-eaters). Their jaws are flexible and loosely connected to their skull so that they can open their mouths wide—and even dislocate (unhinge) their lower jaws—to eat large **prey**.

Snakes can be divided into those that inject venom (poison) into their prey and those that do not. Rear-fangs, pythons, and burrowers do not inject venom.

Rear-fangs snakes

Rear-fangs snakes are the largest snake **family**. They live all over the world and include king snakes, corn, and garter snakes. They get their name because of the large teeth at the back of their jaws, which are used to grip onto prey as they swallow it. Some rear-fangs snakes use their fangs to slit open eggs they have eaten so that they can swallow the contents. A few rear-fangs produce weakly venomous saliva, but they cannot inject it.

King snake—colorful rear fang

- Rear fang—teeth at back of mouth
- Bright colors suggest it is poisonous (it isn't!)
- Prey ranges from frogs to rattlesnakes

Constrictors catch their prey using sharp teeth and then coil their strong body around it to stop it from breathing.

In the loop

Boas and pythons include the largest snakes in the world, such as the anaconda of South America, which measures up to 10 meters (33 feet) long, and the reticulated python of Asia. Some of the reasons they are grouped together are their large belly scales, obvious necks, and flexible upper jaw. Most live in trees, gripping onto branches with their belly scales, but some, like the anaconda, live mostly in water.

Boas and pythons kill large prey—usually **mammals** ranging from rats to deer—by squeezing them to death. This is called constriction. They bite and crush smaller prey in their jaws.

Burrowers

Some families of snakes are grouped together because they are **adapted** for burrowing. Blind snakes have thin, wormlike bodies. They use their hard, blunt head to push through soil, getting a grip using a sharp spine on their tail. They have tiny eyes because they live in dark burrows and find their prey—mainly ants—using their sense of smell. Their scales protect them from ant bites, but some also produce bad smells that repel ants.

Cobras, vipers, and sea snakes inject venom to paralyze (stop movement in) or kill their **prey**. They may also threaten to use venom as a defense if a **predator** tries to attack them. When a snake is close enough to its prey, it strikes by jabbing its fangs into the target and injecting venom. It then pulls its fangs away quickly, because they are fragile and might be damaged. Only after the poison has worked will the snake swallow its prey. Venomous snakes can be classified by the type of teeth they have.

Cobras—fixed fangs

The cobra group includes snakes such as the king cobra, krait, taipan, and mamba. They are grouped together because their fangs are fixed in position in their upper jaw. Fixed-fang snakes are mostly **nocturnal** hunters. Their venom moves down grooves in the fangs into the prey once they have bitten it. Fixed-fang snakes mostly feed on rats, lizards, and frogs.

Rattlesnake—feared predator

- Pit viper—heat-detecting pits on head
- Loosely connected segments at tip of tail rattle when shaken
- Rattle used for defense to frighten predators
- Prey attacked using long, folding, venomous fangs

Vipers—folding fangs

Vipers are classified together because their long, curved fangs are hollow, connected to their venom **glands**, and fold into their mouths. When vipers strike, they fold their fangs down, and large muscles at the back of their diamond-shaped heads pump venom through the fangs into their victim. When not in use, fangs fold up into grooves in their mouths for protection.

Vipers usually ambush their prey. Pit vipers have special pits (holes) on their heads that they use to detect heat given off by **mammals** such as mice when they approach. Young copperheads hide in leaf litter and wag their yellow tail tip so it resembles a worm. They do this to attract worm-eating prey such as frogs.

Sea snakes

One group of snakes is **adapted** for life in shallow **tropical** seawater. Members of this **family** have flattened tails for swimming. They come to the surface to breathe air into their lungs, close valves over their nostrils, and dive for up to five hours. Sea snake venom is generally stronger than other snake venom, so they can paralyze their slippery fish prey quickly before it gets away.

Do you know ... what venom is?

Venom is special spit made in large venom glands in the snake's head. It contains a mixture of chemicals. Some chemicals paralyze or kill the prey, but others **digest** (break down) the prey from the inside.

Sea snakes hunt in holes in coral reefs for fish prey such as eels.

Turtles are among the easiest to recognize of all reptiles. All turtles have shortened bodies covered by a rigid, box-shaped **carapace** (shell). The carapace is a layer of hard, large **scales** covering flat, arched rib bones, which are attached to the backbone. Many turtles also have a tough shell under their belly called a **plastron**.

Turtles have no teeth, although many can bite well. Their jaws are often beak-like and have sharp edges. Most turtles live in shallow fresh water and can hold their breath underwater. Their legs are **adapted** for swimming, either by having a broad, flattened shape (flippers), or by having webbed toes.

Pond turtles

Freshwater turtles form about one-third of all turtle **species**, such as terrapins, painted, bog, and wood turtles. They live in pond, marsh, or estuary **habitats** in Asia and North, South, and Central America. All have hard, domed shells and eat insects, snails, and fish. Box turtles pull in their head, legs, and tail, and raise their plastron to meet their carapace, to form a tight, protective box if attacked by a **predator**.

Red-eared terrapin— common pond dweller

- Freshwater turtle
- Hard, domed shell
- Thick legs with webbed feet good for swimming and walking on land

20

Fearsome turtles

Snapping turtles have very sharp jaws and a thick, ridged shell, which is often covered with growing pondweed. The alligator snapper of the southern United States can weigh 90 kilograms (200 pounds). It has a muscular, wormlike growth, called a lure, on its tongue that it wags to lure inquisitive **prey** such as fish, frogs, or other turtles. Snapping turtles also eat water plants and floating fruit.

A softer side

Softshell turtles have flat, smooth carapaces covered with leathery skin instead of scales. They live in rivers, streams, and wetlands. Soft shells provide less protection than hard shells, but are lighter to carry around. Many of these turtles, such as the Chinese soft-shell, have long necks and noses that they use like snorkels so that they can breathe while remaining mostly hidden underwater.

Alligator snapping turtle— fearsome jaws

- Can hold breath and wait on river bottom for up to an hour
- Lure on tongue attracts prey
- Snaps at prey with large cutting jaws

Side-necked turtles

Most turtles pull their necks right back under their carapace for protection. Side-necked turtles, such as the matamata, are classified in a separate group because they pull in their necks by folding them sideways.

Some turtles are **adapted** for life on dry land. They are called tortoises. Others are adapted for life in the sea. They are called marine turtles.

Tortoises

Tortoises have stubby heads and high, dome-shaped **carapaces** covered with large **scales**. Their feet are shaped like clubs for walking, and they have long, heavy claws for digging in hard ground.

Most are herbivores, which means they feed on plants. Garden tortoises avoid cold seasons by burrowing into leaves and hibernating (sleeping through winter) until it is warm again. Desert tortoises dig burrows up to 12 meters (40 feet) long and return to them to take shelter from hot weather.

Do you know ... how big a tortoise can grow?

Some **species** of tortoises grow to enormous sizes and great ages. The Galapagos Islands in the Pacific Ocean were named after the giant tortoises that live there (*galapago* is Spanish for "giant tortoise"). These giant tortoises can be over 1 meter (3 feet) long, weigh over 225 kilograms (500 pounds), and live for over 100 years. Each island had a different species, with a different shell shape and food type. Many of them have become **extinct** because sailors used the tortoises as easy food in the past. Goats have also stripped the islands of the plant food the tortoises need.

Marine turtles

Two **families** of large turtles live almost their whole lives at sea. Most marine turtles, such as the green turtle or olive ridley sea turtle, have hard, smooth carapaces. The leatherback turtle is classified separately, because its ridged carapace is covered with **cartilage** more like leathery skin than scales. It can reach nearly 3 meters (10 feet) in length and weigh around 500 kilograms (1,100 pounds). It swims over huge areas, feeding on **prey**, such as jellyfish, which it grips using its jagged beak-like jaws and spines inside its throat.

Green turtle—ocean traveler
- Streamlined carapace and **plastron** to move easily through the water
- Grows up to 1.5 m (5 ft) long
- Weighs around 100 to 150 kg (220 to 330 lbs)
- 30 years old before lays eggs
- Migrates 2,000 km (1,250 miles) to lay eggs

Female marine turtles often travel long distances to lay their eggs, going back to the beach where they hatched themselves many years earlier. Scientists think they find their way by sensing Earth's magnetic forces, as if they have a built-in compass. The female drags herself onto the beach, digs a hole, and lays over 200 eggs. Only a few of them will survive and return to the same beach in the future to lay their own eggs.

Crocodiles are massive, heavily armored reptiles grouped in the **order** Crocodilia. There are 23 **species** in the world, including true crocodiles, gharials, alligators, and caimans. Most live in **tropical** rivers and lakes.

All species of crocodile have bodies, heads, and tails that are long and legs that are short. Their thick **scales** are strengthened with bony plates for protection. Some scales are smooth and flat, while others form hard ridges on their backs and tails. Like other reptiles, crocodiles absorb energy from the sun's warmth through their scales when they **bask** on riverbanks.

Catching food

Crocodiles usually hunt **prey**, such as fish, in the water, although they also catch food on land. Crocodiles have eyes and nostrils on top of their heads, so they can see and breathe while keeping their body and the rest of their head hidden underwater. Their long jaws contain at least 60 heavy teeth. Crocodiles have a special flap behind their tongues to stop them from drowning when they open their mouths to catch food underwater. They produce strong stomach juices and swallow stones to help them break food down rapidly. The stones also help them stay submerged underwater.

Crocodiles use their long, muscular tails for swimming rather than their webbed hind feet. This crocodile is sliding into the water after basking in the sun.

True crocodiles

True crocodiles have long and tapering jaws. The fourth tooth from the front of the lower jaw can be seen clearly when their jaws are closed. Members of this **family** live mostly in fresh water, but the saltwater crocodile swims in the sea between the islands where it lives. The largest, the Indopacific crocodile, can reach up to 7 meters (23 feet) in length.

Large crocodiles often catch big **mammals** or birds by surprise. Nile crocodiles wait, hidden, for wildebeest and even lions to come for a drink at a waterhole. They then lunge out of the water, grabbing their prey and pulling it into the water to drown it. They lodge the prey between rocks or tree roots to stop it from moving, grip on with their teeth, and then rotate their whole body to rip bits off to swallow.

Gharials

The gharial, which lives in rivers in India and Nepal, is classified separately from true crocodiles because it has very long, narrow jaws **adapted** to trap its prey—fast-moving, slippery fish. Males have a bulbous end to their snouts, which they use to make their calls louder when they call females during the **mating** season.

Gharials have lots of curved, sharp, interlocking teeth to catch fish with.

Alligators and Caimans

Alligators and caimans are classified separately from crocodiles, although they appear to be very similar. The differences are that their jaws are broader and shorter, and the upper jaw overlaps the lower jaw when their mouths are closed. Also, on each side of an alligator's lower jaw, the fourth tooth fits into a socket on the upper jaw.

Alligator breeding

Alligators are unusual among crocodiles in the care they give to their young. After a female alligator has **mated**, she builds a nest out of plants and mud on a riverbank above the water. She lays about 50 eggs in the nest and covers them carefully. She then stays on guard nearby for around two months as the eggs **incubate**. She does this because many animals, such as monitor lizards and racoons, like to eat the eggs.

When the babies hatch they call out and the mother breaks open the nest. She even helps crack some of her eggs open so that the babies hatch more easily. The babies stay together in a group, and their mother guards them for up to two years, until they are big enough to take care of themselves.

The female American alligator is very protective of her young. She will often **bask** in safety on her back or head.

Caimans

Caimans are close relatives of alligators, but they live in different parts of the world. Caimans live in South American rivers such as the Amazon. They have short skulls, often with ridges down them, and bony, overlapping **scales** on their bellies.

The smallest crocodiles are dwarf caimans. They only grow about 1.5 meters (5 feet) long. They have short, upturned snouts used to dig burrows to take shelter in during the day. They are **nocturnal**, hunting crabs in water and beetles and other insects on land.

Larger caimans eat mainly fish and frogs. The biggest is the black caiman, which can grow up to 6 meters (20 feet) long and eats bigger **prey** such as capybara (a type of giant rodent).

The spectacled caiman gets its name from the bony ridge connecting its eyes, which looks a bit like glasses. Females often share a nest and share the task of caring for each other's babies after the eggs hatch.

Boy or girl?

The eggs of some **species** of reptiles are very sensitive to temperature. In crocodiles, if the nest temperature is high, all of the baby crocodiles will be male. If the temperature is low, they will all be female. In the middle, a mixture of the two sexes will hatch out. In turtles, it is the other way around, with cooler temperatures producing male babies.

The number of different types of living **organisms** in the world is often called **biodiversity**. Sadly, all over the world, **species** of living organisms are becoming **extinct**. This means that these organisms no longer exist on Earth. There are many different reasons for this. Extinction has always happened—some species die out and other species **evolve**. But today people are changing the world in ways that affect all other species.

People are destroying the places where animals live. We are cutting down rain forests and polluting the air and the water. Our use of fossil fuels, such as oil and gas, is causing global warming. Global warming is a rise in Earth's average temperature and a change in weather patterns. When the temperature and the weather change, it can have a serious effect on living things.

Where do YOUR plastic bags end up?

Marine turtles are endangered. Their eggs have been stolen as a special food, the beaches where they lay their eggs have become vacation resorts, and now plastic waste is polluting the seas. Around the world, people use billions of plastic bags every day, and some of this plastic waste is dumped in the oceans. A jellyfish and a water-filled plastic bag look very similar underwater. Thousands of marine turtles are dying because they have eaten plastic bags, which they cannot **digest** and which block their intestines.

Many types of reptiles have remained relatively unchanged for thousands of years. However, with the changes in the environment that are taking place, many reptiles may not survive for you to show your grandchildren!

Reptiles have been on Earth a long time. The earliest reptile **fossils** are over 300 million years old. The dinosaurs were reptiles. They included an amazing range of species, many of which appear to have survived almost unchanged since prehistoric times. It would be a tragedy if these ancient species were to disappear now.

This Southern Tenerife lizard is used as a **bioindicator**. If levels of toxic chemicals build up in the insects it feeds on, the number of lizards will fall as they are poisoned. Lots of lizards mean a healthy environment.

What can be done?

To help prevent reptiles from becoming extinct, people need to take better care of Earth. If global warming can be stopped, many species will be saved. It is important to protect the places where reptiles live. Biodiversity is important—we need as many species of reptiles as possible for the future.

Glossary

adaptation special features that help living things to survive in their habitat

bask get warm in the sun

biodiversity different types of organisms around the world

bioindicator when the health of a particular organism reveals what state the environment is in

camouflage color, shape, or pattern that disguises an animal against its background

carapace hard shell

cartilage flexible skeleton material

cell smallest unit of life

class classification grouping. Each class is divided into orders.

digest break down food for use by the body

ectotherm term describing animals that cannot control their own body temperature, so they are always as hot or cold as their surroundings

evolve change over time

extinct when a species has died out and no longer exists

family classification grouping. Vipers are a family of snakes.

fossil remains of organisms that once lived on Earth

gene structure by which all living things pass on characteristics to the next generation

genus (plural **genera**) classification grouping. Each genus is divided into species.

gland place in an animal's body that secretes particular fluids

habitat place where organisms live

incubation keeping eggs at the right temperature for the babies to develop

kingdom in classification, the largest grouping of living things (for example, animals)

mammal class of animals. Mammals are endothermic (make their own heat) and usually hairy. Their babies grow inside the mother, who suckles them and cares for them after they are born.

mate when a male fertilizes a female so that her eggs start to develop into babies

nocturnal active at night

order classification grouping. There are four orders within the class of reptile.

organ part of the body with a specific job to do, such as the liver or heart

organism living thing

phylum (plural **phyla**) classification grouping. Each phylum is divided into classes.

plastron lower shell of a turtle

predator animal that hunts and eats other animals

prey animal hunted and eaten by another animal

reproduce give birth to babies

scales overlapping or interlocking pieces that form a protective layer over reptile skin

species classification grouping. A green iguana is a species of iguana.

tropical living in parts of the world near the equator (tropics)

vertebrate animal with an internal skeleton of bone or cartilage

Find Out More

Books

McCarthy, Colin. *Eyewitness: Snake*. New York: Dorling Kindersley, 2000.

McNab, Chris. *Nature's Monsters: Endangered Reptiles*. Milwaukee: Gareth Stevens, 2006.

Pyers, Greg. *Classifying Animals: Why Am I a Reptile?* Chicago: Raintree, 2006.

Snedden, Robert. *Living Things: Reptiles*. Mankato, Minn.: Smart Apple Media, 2009.

Websites

http://kids.yahoo.com/animals/reptiles
On this web page there are lots of links to information about individual reptiles.

www.mnh.si.edu
This is the website of the National Museum of Natural History in Washington, D.C.

http://nationalzoo.si.edu/Animals/ReptilesAmphibians/ForKids/
This web page of the Smithsonian National Zoological Park in Washington, D.C., has fact sheets and games about all kinds of reptiles.

www.sandiegozoo.org/animalbytes/a-reptiles.html
This web page of the San Diego Zoo offers more information about reptiles.

Index